TinkerActive

EARLY SKILLS WORKBOOKS

Ages **4+**

Motor Control

written by **Enil Sidat**

educational consulting by **Casey Federico, MSEd**

illustrated by **Karen Wall**

odd dot

NEW YORK

120 Broadway
New York, NY 10271
OddDot.com

Copyright © 2023 by Odd Dot

By purchasing this workbook, the buyer is permitted to reproduce pages for classroom use only, but not for commercial resale. Please contact the publisher for permission to reproduce pages for an entire school or school district. With the exception of the above, no portion of this book may be reproduced—mechanically, electronically, or by any other means, including photocopying—without written permission of the publisher.

ISBN: 978-1-250-78438-4

WRITER Enil Sidat

ILLUSTRATOR Karen Wall

EDUCATIONAL CONSULTANT Casey Federico, MSEd

CHARACTER DESIGNER Anna-Maria Jung

DESIGNERS Kayleigh McCann and Caitlyn Hunter

EDITORS Nathalie Le Du and Peter Mavrikis

Our books may be purchased in bulk for promotional, educational, or business use. Please contact your local bookseller or the Macmillan Corporate and Premium Sales Department at (800) 221-7945 ext. 5442 or by email at MacmillanSpecialMarkets@macmillan.com.

DISCLAIMER
The publisher and author disclaim responsibility for any loss, injury, or damages caused as a result of any of the instructions described in this book.

TinkerActive is a trademark of Odd Dot.

Printed in China by Hung Hing Off-set Printing Co. Ltd.,
Heshan City, Guangdong Province

First edition, 2023

1 3 5 7 9 10 8 6 4 2

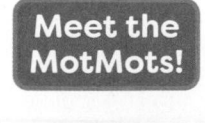
Meet the MotMots!

Amelia

Brian

Callie

Dimitri

Enid

Frank

Coloring with Crayons

Tinker Town has a brand-new fire station! Amelia wants to paint the fire station doors red. Color the fire station doors.

1

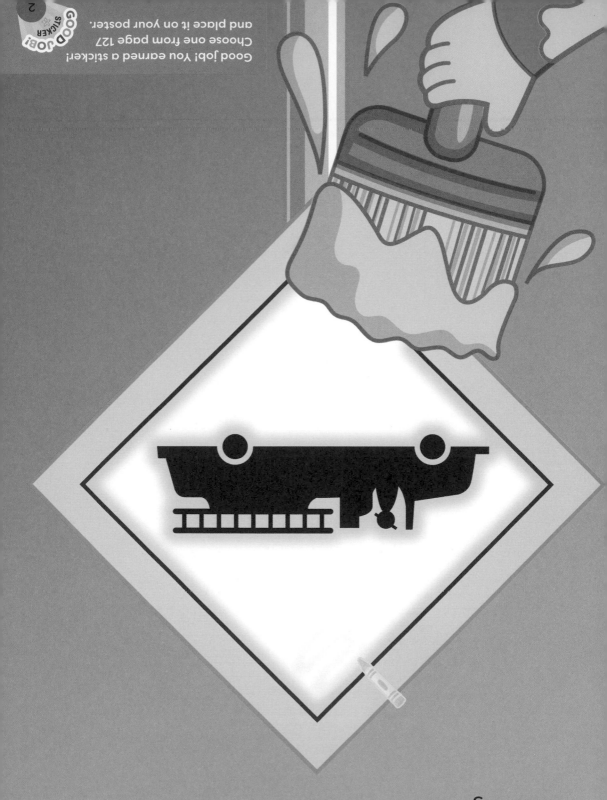

Amelia is all done with the doors! Now color the fire station sign.

Good job! You earned a sticker! Choose one from page 127 and place it on your poster.

GOOD JOB! STICKER GOOD JOB! 2

Brian loves all the lights on the fire truck!
Color the headlights.

★ HEY, GROWN-UPS! ★

We've created spaces with large buffers so your child won't worry about coloring outside the lines. For now, your child is just getting comfortable with learning to fill in spaces. Encourage your child to color the white space and don't worry about perfection.

GOOD JOB! STICKER 4

Brian wants more lights! Color the warning lights.

Callie checks the fire truck's controls.
Color the controls with their matching colors.

Callie checks the gauges on the fire truck.

Color the gauges with their matching colors.

GREAT WORK!
STICKER

Dimitri is testing the fire hydrant. Color the .

EXCELLENT! STICKER

Dimitri releases water from the fire hydrant. Draw water spraying from the

It's Enid's turn to make the firefighters' dinner.

Color in the vegetables.

★ HEY, GROWN-UPS! ★

In the following pages you might notice that the spaces for coloring are getting smaller and the shapes are getting more irregular. Keep encouraging your child to color these shapes, even when the color goes outside the lines. If they need more practice, try coloring larger spaces on the write-and-wipe game board.

It's Frank's turn to feed the dog. Color the dog dish.

★ HEY, GROWN-UPS!

You might notice that we have removed the buffers around the coloring areas. Encourage your child to stay within the lines when they can, and notice their efforts!

Frank drew a picture of a dog. Complete the picture by coloring the spots on the dog black.

The MotMots get a call and jump in the fire truck! Color their uniforms so they stand out.

GREAT WORK! STICKER

Let's TINKER!

Gather these tools and materials.

Tinker with your materials. **Roll** the crayons. **Rub** them across the paper plates. What do you notice about your crayons and paper plates? Make shapes with them, like a square or a triangle.

Paper plates

Scissors
(with an adult's help)

Crayons

Sticker on page 128

★ HEY, GROWN-UPS! ★

By engaging in make-believe, your child is working on symbolic thinking and growing their creative skills. Encourage them by joining the fun!

Let's MAKE! A Firefighter Hat!

1. Color a paper plate red.

2. With the help of an adult, **cut** a semicircle along the inside of the rim.

●●●▶

3. Fold the front of the hat up.

4. Place the sticker from page 128. You've made a firefighter hat!

Place the sticker from page 128.

★ **HEY, GROWN-UPS!** ★

You can find all the stickers at the end of this book. Peeling stickers is great practice for improving fine motor control. If your child has difficulty at first, peel up one corner and ask them to remove the sticker the rest of the way. Your child will gradually develop the skills to peel and place stickers on their own!

Let's **ENGINEER** a solution!

Amelia wants to make a different shape for her hat, but she doesn't know where to start! How can Amelia plan a different shape? **Design** your own hat with a special shape and color.

You're a TinkerActive CHAMPION!

You've earned an extra-special sticker. Peel it and place it anywhere you'd like on your poster.

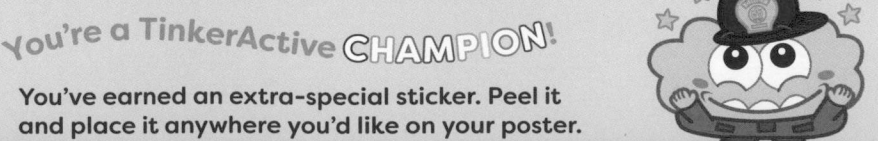

Mazes with a Crayon

Amelia is driving to the police station.

Write a line from the 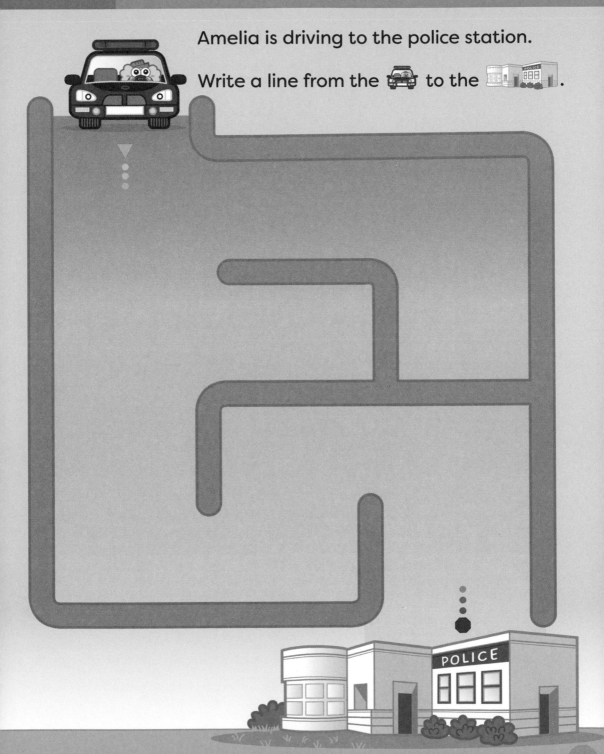 to the .

Amelia is delivering sandwiches to her friends!

Write a line from  to the .

WELL DONE! STICKER

Brian is helping his GrandMotMot cross the street.

Write a line from to the 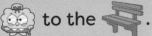.

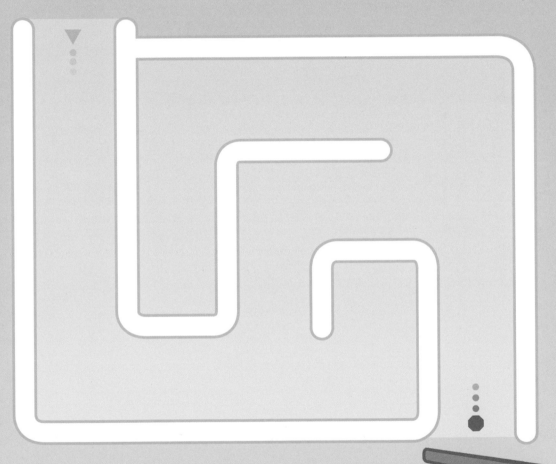

★ HEY, GROWN-UPS! ★

Encourage your child as they advance from the skill of coloring with a crayon to writing lines. This is a big step for a little kid! They are well on their way to learning how to write letters.

Brian is directing the MotTots across the street!
Write a line from the  to the .

18

Callie directs traffic around a broken-down car.

Write a line from the  to the 🚧.

ROAD CLOSED

STOP

★ HEY, GROWN-UPS! ★

Help your child navigate the maze with their finger before using the crayon. It is okay if they go outside the path. Encouraging your child's effort rather than their result is a great way to teach persistence.

The car is fixed! Callie waves to the car as it drives away.
Write a line from the  to the .

Dimitri and Amelia are helping a cat stuck in a tree.

Write a line from the to .

21

Dimitri can't believe it. Now he has to help get Frank's alligator down from the roof!

Write a line from the  to .

Enid is training on the driving course!

Write a line from the 🚓 to the ⚑.

★ HEY, GROWN-UPS! ★

You can make a game of drawing mazes for your child on the write-and-wipe game board. Encourage them by drawing a cartoon of you both running through your specially designed maze toward a favorite place or treat!

BE PROUD! STICKER

24

Enid advances to the harder course!
Write a line from the 🚗 to the 🏁.

Frank is training a service dog on an obstacle course!

Write a line from the  to the 🚩.

YOU DID IT!
STICKER

Frank wants to run a course, too!
Write a line from 🏁 to the ⌐.

The MotMots help people stay safe at the Tinker Town Parade!

Write a line from  to the .

GOOD JOB! STICKER

28

Enid has lost her favorite toy!
Write a line from  to the  .

Gather these tools and materials.

Roll, spin, and toss your marbles. Are they all the same size or different? Are some rougher and some smoother? Are the marbles wider than the craft sticks?

Shoebox

Scissors
(with an adult's help)

Craft sticks

Glue

Marbles

Marker

Let's **MAKE!**

A Shoebox Marble Drop!

1. With the help of an adult, **poke** the craft sticks through the shoebox. Use the scissors to cut a hole first if needed.

2. Cut holes into the top of the box for the marbles to drop through.

3. You've made a marble drop! **Place** a marble into one of the holes at the top and see it fall! What happens if you tilt the box?

Let's **ENGINEER** a solution!

Frank is showing his stuffed animals the marble drop. He wants to keep track of where the marbles land most often. What can he use to keep track?

croc
bear
bunny
monkey

Mazes with a Pencil

Enid fell and hurt her leg! Amelia drives to reach her.

Write a line from the  to .

WELL DONE! STICKER

★ **HEY, GROWN-UPS!**

Transitioning from crayon to a regular pencil can be a challenge. That's why we encourage you to start with colored pencils as a great middle step. Ask your child which they prefer: crayons, colored pencils, or regular pencils. Using what they prefer will encourage more practice, and that's what they need most!

Amelia drives back to the hospital.

Write a line from the  to the 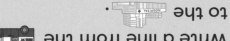 to the 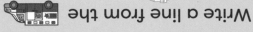 .

Brian rolls the stretcher to get the patient.

Write a line from the  to the .

Brian pushes the patient to an open room.

Write a line from ![stretcher] to the ![elevator].

★ HEY, GROWN-UPS! ★

We've made the paths of this maze narrower, and it's all right if your child goes outside the walls a bit. Encourage them to find their way back onto the path as they go. The important skill is gaining comfort writing in narrower and narrower paths as they progress in their fine motor skills!

Callie checks the X-ray!

Write a line from the ▷ to the ⬡.

Callie compares the X-ray to a map of the skeletal system. Write a line from the ▶ to the ⬡.

★ HEY, GROWN-UPS! ★

If your child is enjoying the mazes, try using the write-and-wipe game board to create a maze together. Ask them how many turns they want in the maze, how many dead ends, and how many split paths. Let them describe as you draw the first few mazes. Then change roles and have your child draw a maze for you to try out!

GOOD JOB! STICKER

Dimitri helps Enid with her exercises!
Write a line from the ▶ to the ⬣.

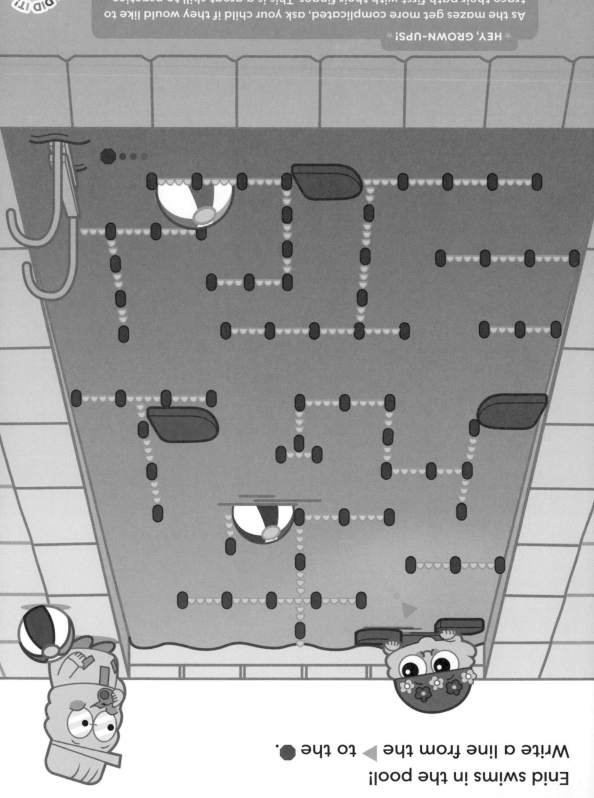

Enid swims in the pool!
Write a line from the ▶ to the ⬡.

YOU DID IT! STICKER

HEY, GROWN-UPS!

As the mazes get more complicated, ask your child if they would like to trace their path first with their finger. This is a great skill to practice. Then they can use the pencil when they've charted their route!

Amelia is helping in the nursery ward.
She walks quietly to get the baby a hat.

Write a line from the ▷ to the ⬡.

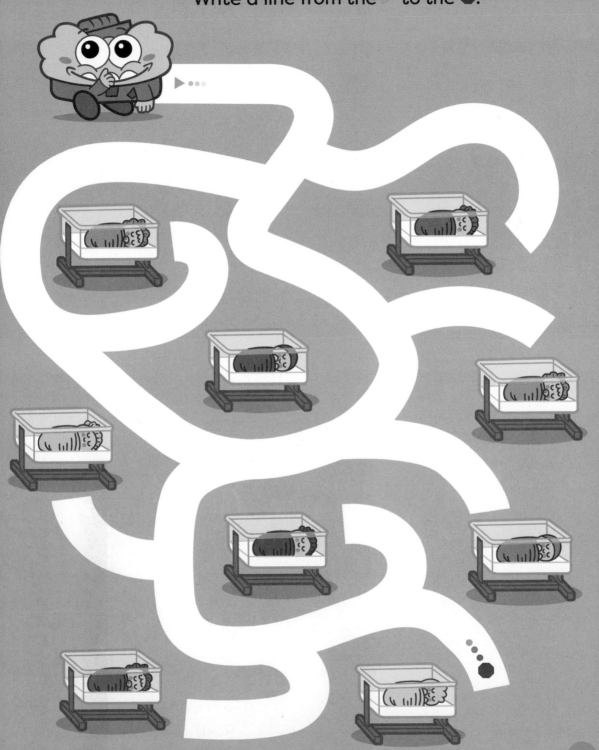

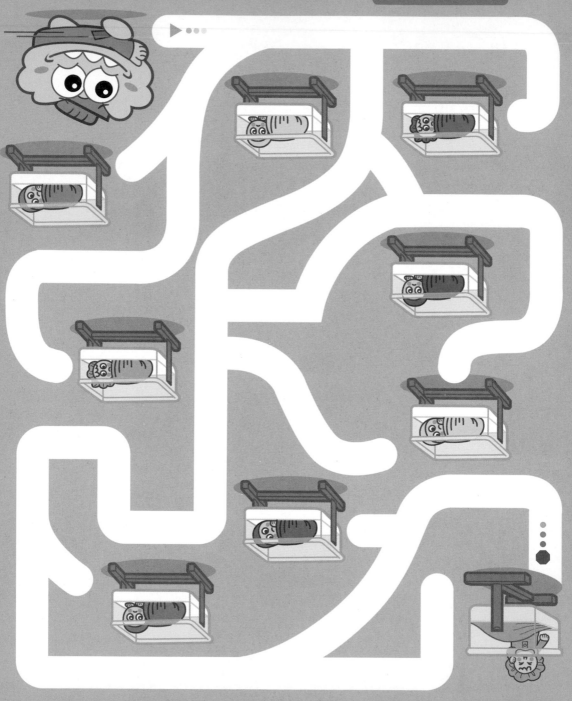

★ **HEY, GROWN-UPS!**

Make a maze for your child outside with chalk. First, draw small mazes for them to complete by tracing their fingers along the path, or using a toy car. Then draw a real maze for them to walk through!

A baby is crying! Run back!
Write a line from the ⬡ to the ●.

Frank ate a lot of candy and has a bellyache.

Write a line from to the .

EXCELLENT! STICKER

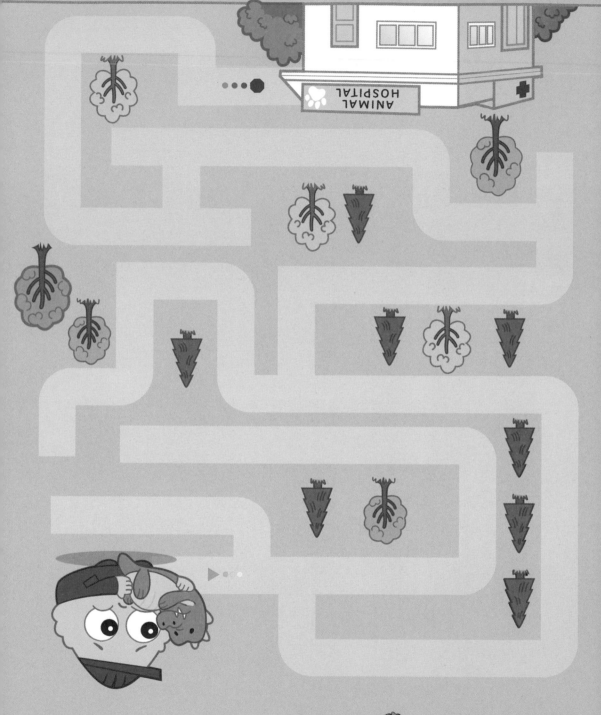

ANIMAL HOSPITAL

Frank's alligator ate a lot of candy, too.
Write a line from 🐹 to the 🚐.

The MotMots are bringing flowers to Enid.
Write a line from the ▶ to the ⬢.

★ HEY, GROWN-UPS! ★

These mazes are a great opportunity to play story time. As your child travels along the path, ask about the characters they see. What are the characters saying? What are they doing? When your child reaches the end, praise their work by telling them they completed the story.

Enid is all better and is going home!
Write a line from the ▶ to the ⬣.

GREAT WORK! STICKER

Let's **TINKER!**

Gather these tools and materials.

Before you turn the page, **tinker** with your materials. Are the straws straight or curved? How many straws fit on the cardboard, end to end? How does the marble roll on the cardboard?

Straws

Scissors
(with an adult's help)

Cardboard

Glue

Marble

★ HEY, GROWN-UPS! ★

As your child plays with the materials, ask them about what they observe. If the marble keeps falling off the cardboard, ask how they can modify the cardboard to keep the marble on. (Hint: You can use plastic wrap to enclose the marble run.)

Let's **MAKE!**

Marble Maze!

1. With the help of an adult, **cut** the straws into different lengths.

● ● ● ▶

2. **Arrange** them on the cardboard surface to make a maze. Make sure that the paths you create are wide enough for your marble.

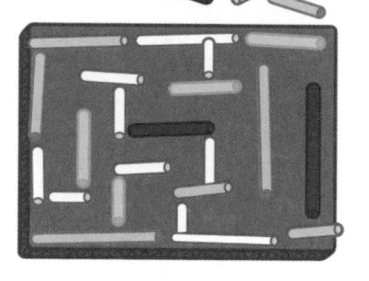

3. **Glue down** the straw pieces.

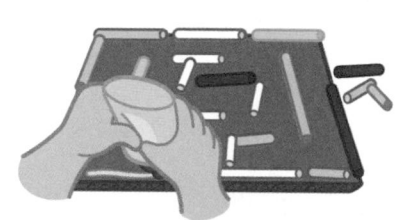

4. **Place** the marble on the surface and roll it around the path. You've made a marble maze!

Let's **ENGINEER** a solution!

Enid and Dimitri are working together to create a corn maze for the Tinker Town Fall Festival! How can they plan a challenging maze? Use the write-and-wipe game board to **design** a maze with the most dead ends. Then try to build it with your straws and cardboard.

You're a TinkerActive CHAMPION!

Amelia is planting trees with the parks department.
Write a line from each ▶ to its ●.

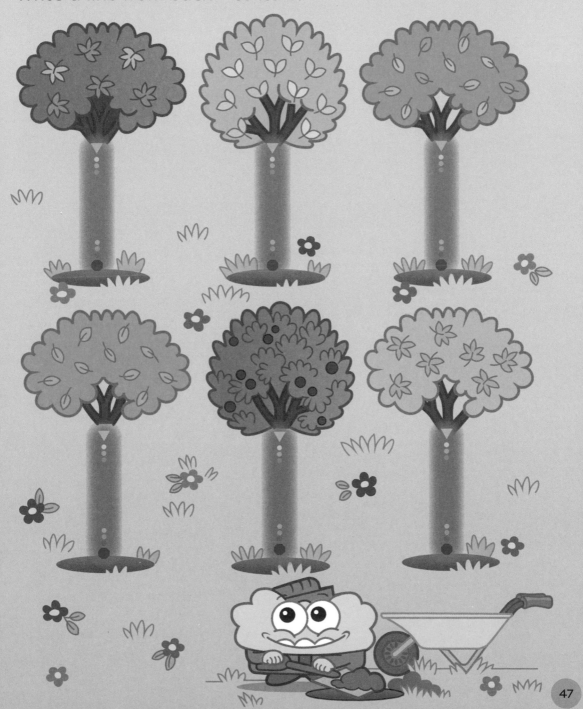

EXCELLENT! STICKER

★ **HEY, GROWN-UPS!**

Encourage your child to stay on the dotted line. It is all right if your child isn't very accurate just yet. They are learning a lot at once: how to hold a pencil, how to control their lines, and how to create more and more complicated lines. As the section progresses, they will get more familiar with the exercise and more comfortable with their pencil.

Amelia is making flower beds.
Trace the line from each ◀ to its ●.

Brian is building the seesaws for the playground.
Write a line from each ▶ to its ●.

Brian has found a friend to play with!
Trace the line from each ▶ to its ●.

Callie is building a swing set.
Write a line from each ▶ to its ●.

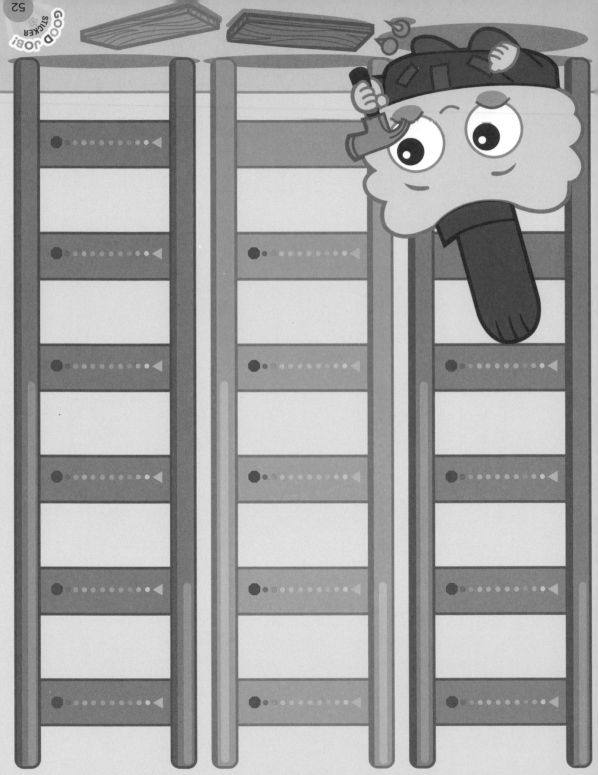

GOOD JOB! STICKER

Now Callie is assembling the ladders for the slides.
Trace the line from each ▶ to its ●.

Dimitri places the boards in the fence for the dog park.
Write a line from each ▶ to its ●.

★ HEY, GROWN-UPS! ★

This is a great time to go back to the beginning of this book and see all the progress
your child has made in learning how to hold a pencil, how to control their lines, and
how to create increasingly complicated lines. Congratulate them on their effort!

The dogs are ready to play! Dimitri paints the fence to make it look nice.

Trace the line from each > to its ●.

EXCELLENT! STICKER

Enid is mowing around the bushes so she can play in the field later.

Write a line from each ▶ to its ●.

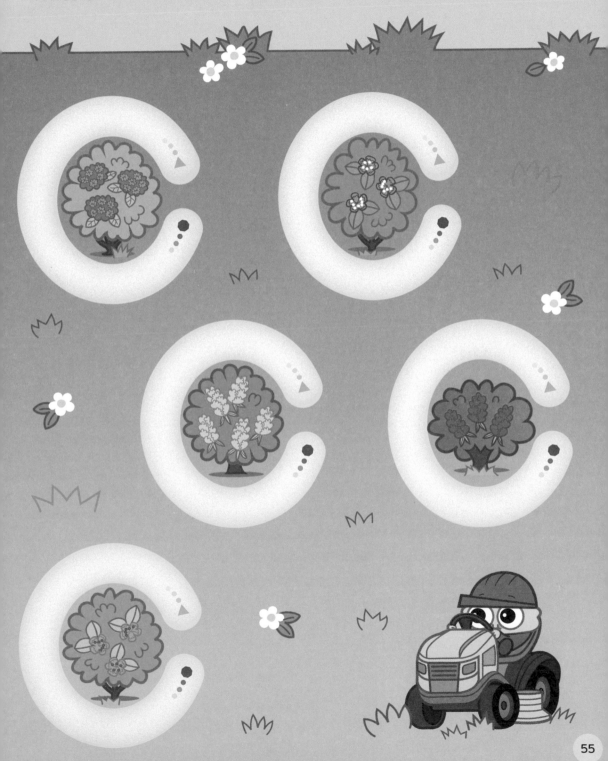

Enid is playing Frisbee.
Trace the line from each ▶ to its ⬡.

Frank blows bubbles in the park!
Write a line from each ▶ to its ●.

GOOD JOB!
STICKER
58

HEY, GROWN-UPS!

The longer the tracing line, the more challenging it may be for your child to stay on the line. Encourage your child to try and try again with different colored pencils and phrases like "Keep going!" or "I'm proud of the way you are building your skills!"

Frank has to get back to work shoveling mulch.
Trace the line from each ▶ to its ●.

After a long day of work, the MotMots sit by the pond in the park. Some of the MotMots like to spend time fishing.

Write a line from each ▶ to its ●.

But they can't sit still for long. The MotMots play tag around the beautiful park!

Trace the line from each ▶ to its ●.

Let's **TINKER!**

Hold the different materials in your hands. Are the erasers on the pencils hard or soft? Are they flat along the top?

Paper

Pencils with erasers

Paintbrush

Paint

Let's **MAKE!**   Handprint Tree!

1. **Place** your hand and arm on the paper and spread your fingers.

2. Use a pencil to **trace** the outline of your hand.

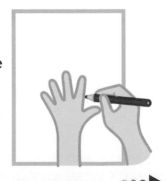

●●●▶

61

3. **Paint** your handprint brown.

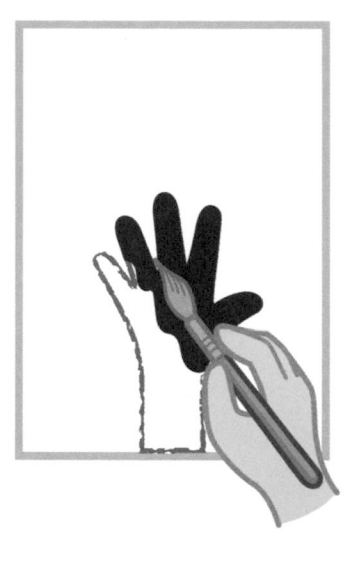

4. **Press** pencil erasers into the paint and **stamp** colored leaves in the tree.

Let's ENGINEER a solution!

Brian is painting a mural in the park. But he doesn't know what else to paint. **Find** other objects around your house to trace, and draw things you would find at a park, like flowers or a fountain.

You're a TinkerActive CHAMPION!

Stickering

The MotMots are helping at the animal rescue fair! Amelia decorates the banner.

Sticker the onto the banner.

ANIMAL RESCUE FAIR

Amelia bought balloons, but they blew away!

Sticter the  onto the sky.

ANIMAL RESCUE FAIR

★ HEY, GROWN-UPS! ★

Peeling stickers is great practice for improving fine motor control. Don't worry about the orientation of the stickers, or if they bubble or overlap as your child places them. The goal, at first, is for your child to master the simple act of applying the sticker to a sheet of paper. Watch as they progress quickly!

GREAT WORK! STICKER

Brian is arranging tasty pet treats on the table.

Sticker the treats onto the table.

Brian is labeling the pet play areas. Sticker the signs to match the animals in each pen.

★ HEY, GROWN-UPS! ★

Encourage your child to place the stickers in the space provided, but don't worry if the stickers are crooked or upside down when compared to the background. Ask them about the animals and what they are doing. What does your child see? What do they imagine the animals doing?

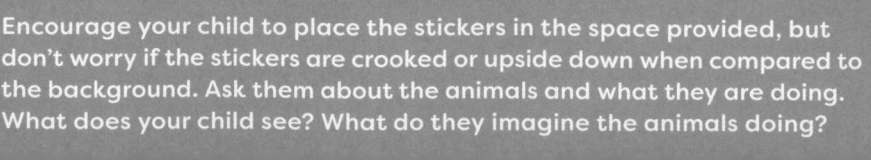

WELL DONE!
STICKER

66

Callie is bringing empty animal carriers to the fair for new pet owners!

Sticker the   onto the van.

Callie has arrived at the fair! She delivers the carriers to each table.

Sticker the  onto the tables.

Dimitri hands over puppies to loving families.
Make sure they hold the pups right side up!

Sticker the  next to each family.

Dimitri gives the kittens to families to hold, too.
He uses gloves so he doesn't get scratched!
Sticker the  next to each family.

Enid drives up with the fish tank. The fish tank can hold many different fish. Sticker the  onto the fish tank.

★ HEY, GROWN-UPS! ★

Instruct your child to hold the sticker above the page and turn it around until they think it's just right. Then have them place it. Say something like "I really like how you think about where you want the sticker to go before you place it."

Enid also brought a shark and an octopus!

Sticker the  and the onto the fish tank.

EXCELLENT! STICKER

Frank brought hats
for all the new pets!

Sticker the hats
onto the pets.

The other MotMots
want hats, too!

Sticker the hats on
the MotMots.

GOOD JOB!
STICKER

All the MotMots now have a pet.

Sticker the pets next to each MotMot.

Everyone who takes a pet home gets a ribbon!
Sticker the  on each MotMot.

Gather these tools and materials.

Examine your materials. Are the craft sticks rough or smooth? Do your markers write well on the craft sticks?

Craft sticks

Markers

Stickers
(see page 129)

Let's **MAKE!**

Sticker Puppets!

1. **Color** your craft sticks using the markers.

2. **Find** the animal stickers on page 129.

77

3. Place the face of each animal on the tip of a craft stick.

4. Flip over your craft stick, and carefully place the back of each animal against the first sticker. You're ready for a puppet show!

★ HEY, GROWN-UPS! ★

This craft is designed to be open-ended to encourage your child to use their imagination and express themselves. You can even use the write-and-wipe game board to draw a setting for the animals to play on, or use the animals to trace the mazes in this book.

Let's ENGINEER a solution!

Amelia wants to open a restaurant for her pets. But she doesn't know where to start. **Think** about different items in a restaurant: tables, food, decorations. What can you build with your materials and objects from your home?

You're a TinkerActive CHAMPION!

Amelia is collecting the trash.
Cut along each driveway to
its  to collect the trash.

WELL DONE!
STICKER
80

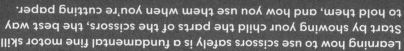

★ HEY, GROWN-UPS! ★

Learning how to use scissors safely is a fundamental fine motor skill.
Start by showing your child the parts of the scissors, the best way
to hold them, and how you use them when you're cutting paper.

Brian is sorting the recycling.
Cut along each of the conveyors.

METAL

PLASTIC

PAPER

GOOD JOB!
STICKER
82

★ HEY, GROWN-UPS!

This is a great opportunity to ask your child to think about all the ways they can hold the paper to make it easier and safer to cut. Most children find it easier to cut upward. Try tearing this activity page out of the book and holding it vertically. Is it easier for your child to cut?

Callie plows each pile of trash toward the garbage pile.
Cut a path from each  to the larger garbage pile.

Dimitri's trash robot got stuck on a tire.

Cut the  out of its mouth to free it.

BE PROUD!
STICKER

★ HEY, GROWN-UPS! ★

Changing direction as you cut is a big jump in difficulty. It's all right if your child wants to cut in separate and noncontinuous lines against the directional arrow, first along one side, and then the other. Encourage their practice and they'll improve in no time!

Enid places the bottles on a conveyor belt.
Cut along each path.

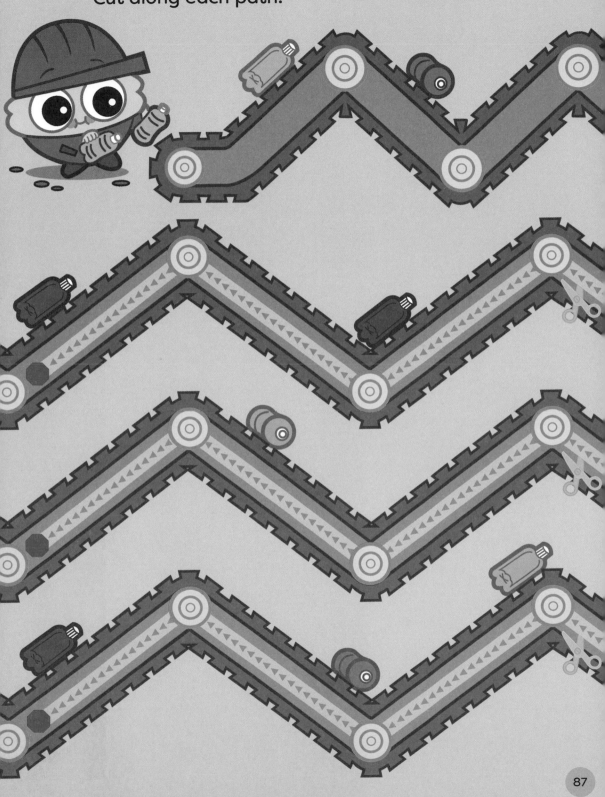

Frank is playing tag with the trash robot!
Cut along each path.

The MotMots are collecting trash for recycling.

Cut out the .

Gather these tools and materials.

Play with your materials. Is your tin can empty or full? Does it have a label? What shape is it?

Tin can
(unopened)

Markers or crayons

Construction paper

Scissors
(with an adult's help)

Glue

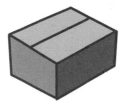

Box

Let's **MAKE!**   Trash Robot!

1. **Remove** the label from the tin can.

2. **Draw** eyes, a mouth, and robot parts on the construction paper. **Look** at the illustrations for inspiration!

••• ▶

3. With the help of an adult, **cut out** the eyes, mouth, and robot parts.

4. Glue them onto the can. You've made a trash robot!

★ **HEY, GROWN-UPS!** ★

You can extend this activity by searching around the house for additional items to glue to your trash robot!

Let's ENGINEER a solution!

Dimitri wants to build the ultimate trash-collecting, recycling, and compacting machine! **Think** of what his robot will need to be the best trash robot it can be. Does it need long arms? Shovel hands? Two mouths? **Cut out** or gather materials for your very best design ideas to make a robot of your own!

You're a TinkerActive CHAMPION!

Using Glue

Brian is replacing the old street signs.

Cut out the old △ from the area below.
Then glue them into the bed of the truck.

★ **HEY, GROWN-UPS!** ★

Using glue is a *big* step for a little kid, especially when it's liquid glue.
Help them by showing the parts of the glue bottle, and how quickly it flows!

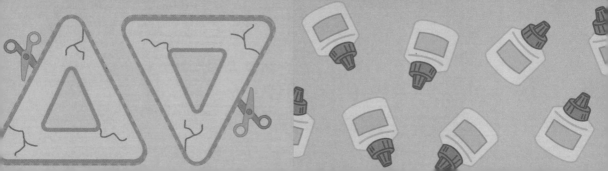

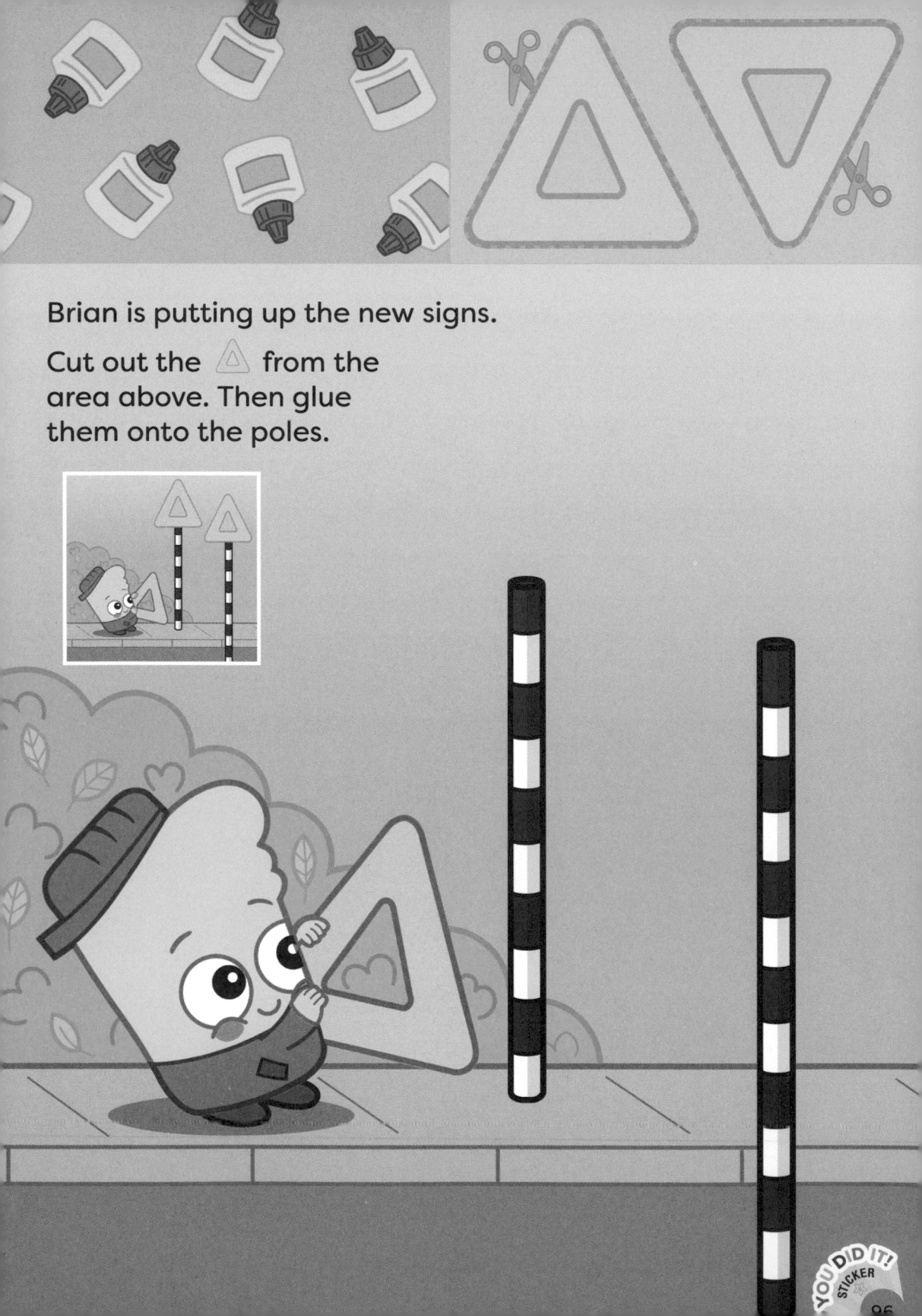

Brian is putting up the new signs.

Cut out the ⚠ from the area above. Then glue them onto the poles.

YOU DID IT! STICKER

Amelia and Dimitri are repairing the road.

Cut out a piece of  from the area below. Then glue it over the pothole.

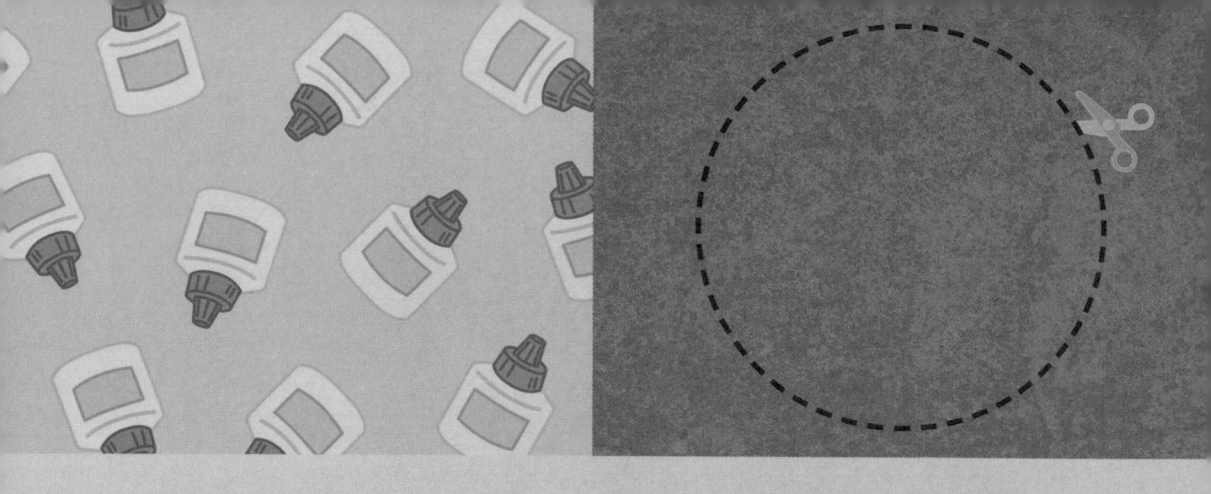

Now Amelia and Dimitri are ready to pour the concrete.

Cut out a piece of ⬤ from the area above. Then glue it over the gravel.

ROAD CLOSED

★ HEY, GROWN-UPS! ★

We practiced cutting with scissors in the previous chapter, but it's okay if your child is still learning how to cut. Circles can be a challenge, so encourage them in the first part of this exercise as they cut out the piece.

Callie is repairing a house. Cut out the  from the area below. Then glue it into the frame.

Now Callie installs the windows beside the door.

Cut out the from the area above.
Then glue it into place.

★ HEY, GROWN-UPS! ★

Using glue in a bottle is messier than using a glue stick, but try a glue bottle when you can! Squeezing a glue bottle helps build grip strength and develop fine motor control.

WELL DONE!
STICKER

Dimitri is fixing the stones on the walking bridge. Cut out the  from the area below. Then glue them to the bridge.

Dimitri sits on the bridge and feeds the ducks.

Cut out the  from the area above.
Then glue them right side
up in the pond.

GOOD JOB!
STICKER

Enid is replacing the bricks on Tinker Town's main avenue.

Cut out the [ ] from the area below. Then glue them to the road.

Once she's finished, Enid wants to play!

Cut out the numbered squares from the area above. Then glue them in place.

Frank is painting a mural of himself as a famous town leader. Cut out the  and the from the area below. Then glue them to the mural.

Frank also paints his trusty sidekick alligator.
Cut out the 👀 and the 🦷 from the
area above. Then glue them in place.

GOOD JOB!
STICKER

The MotMots are placing posters for the sculpture fair all over Tinker Town.

Cut out the  from the area below. Then glue them right side up on any of the walls in town.

CULPTURE FAIR

SCULPTURE FAIR

SCULPTURE FAIR

The MotMots attend the sculpture fair!

Cut out the sculptures from the area above. Then glue them right side up on the pedestals.

WELL DONE! STICKER

Let's TINKER!

Gather these tools and materials.

Let's **experiment** with your new materials! **Pour** some glue into a bowl. Does it flow like water, or is it thick? Use the cotton swabs to stir. Tear some paper and dip it in the glue. What can you stick the paper to?

Cotton swabs

Glue

Construction paper

Tennis ball (or other small ball)

Let's MAKE!

A Tinker Town Sculpture!

1. Glue three cotton swabs together to form a triangle.

2. Make five more triangles using cotton swabs.

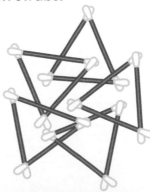

●●●▶

3. **Glue** all six triangles down on the construction paper to make a hexagonal base.

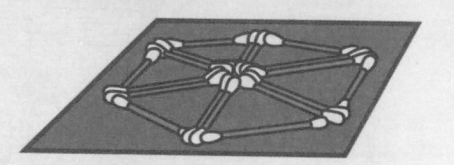

---

4. Now **build** upward using additional triangle shapes to create your own Tinker Town sculpture!

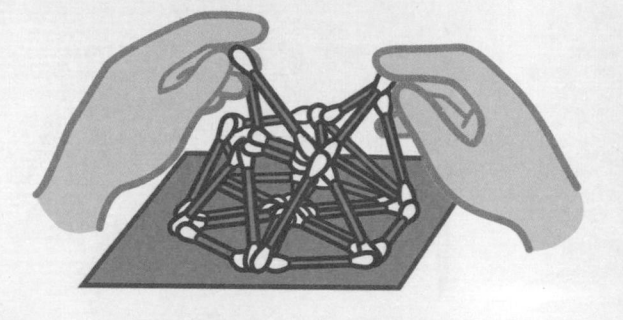

★ HEY, GROWN-UPS! ★

As your child applies the glue to the cotton swabs, help them by holding the pieces together until the glue sets.

Let's ENGINEER a solution!

Enid wants to climb her sculpture, but she doesn't know if it will hold her weight. Can you **design** a cotton-swab sculpture that will hold up a tennis ball?

You're a TinkerActive CHAMPION!

Simple Paper Crafts

Amelia is writing a letter to Brian. Make and decorate the envelope!

Step 1: Cut along the pink dashed lines – – – –.

Step 2: Fold upward along the blue dotted lines ∙∙∙∙∙∙∙∙∙.

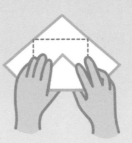

I DREW US!

YOUR FRIEND A x

Fold blue dotted lines ▪▪▪▪▪▪▪ **upward.**

Fold orange dotted lines ▪▪▪▪▪▪▪ **downward.**

Step 3: Place the sticker from page 129 on the envelope to seal it.

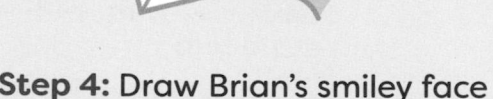

Step 4: Draw Brian's smiley face on the front of the envelope.

Callie is waiting for the mail plane!

Fold the plane so that it can deliver mail.

Step 1: Use a sheet of paper (8 ½ x 11 inches).

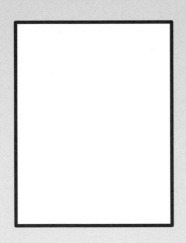

Step 2: Fold sheet in half lengthwise.

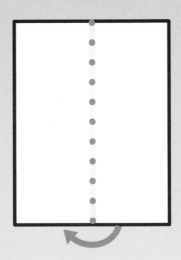

Step 3: Fold the top corners downward toward center.

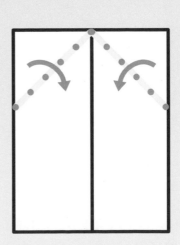

★ **HEY, GROWN-UPS!** ★

After your child makes a fold, show them how to create a crease by dragging your finger along the edge of the paper.

Step 4: Fold the top corners downward toward the middle crease.

Step 5: Fold the paper in half.

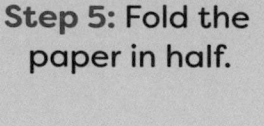

Step 6: Fold both wings downward.

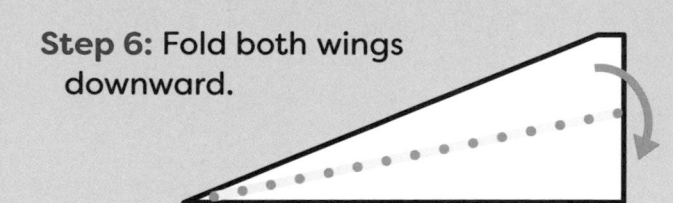

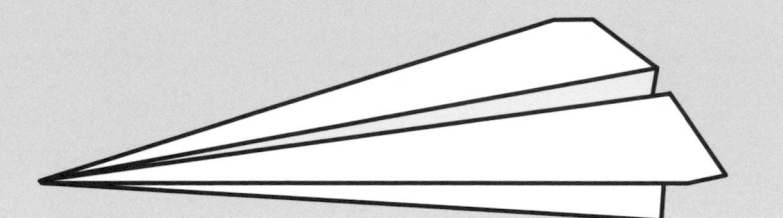

Dimitri is receiving a message from a carrier pigeon!
Fold the pigeon and try balancing it on your finger.

Step 1: Cut along the – – – – –.

Step 2: Fold the body downward along the
–•–•–•– and upward along the ·······.

Step 3: Fold over and glue down the tips of
the wings, indicated by matching glue tabs.

Enid got a lot of presents in the mail.
She's dancing with joy!

Step 1: Cut along the - - - - -.

Step 2: Roll section A into a cylinder, and glue the ends where they overlap.

Step 3: Roll section B tightly, and then glue it to the inside bottom of section A as shown.

B

A

GOOD JOB! STICKER

Step 4: Fold downward along the ·······

Frank is making Frank-shaped bookmarks.

Step 1: Cut along the - - - - -.

Step 2: Fold **A** upward along the ·······.

Step 3: Fold **B** upward along the ········ and glue the tab into its matching place.

Step 4: Add your own drawings on Frank's face by giving him glasses or big teeth!

A   B

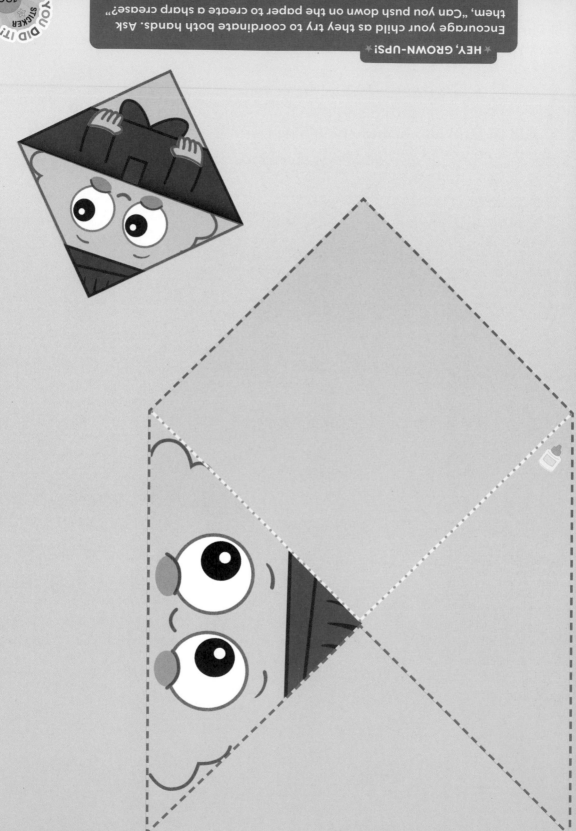

YOU DID IT! STICKER

★ HEY, GROWN-UPS! ★

Encourage your child as they try to coordinate both hands. Ask them, "Can you push down on the paper to create a sharp crease?"

The MotMots are trying to get rid of the junk mail.
Frank's alligator looks hungry.

Step 1: Cut along the - - - - -.

Step 2: Fold upward along
the ·······.

Step 3: Fold downward along
the ·······.

GOOD JOB! STICKER 122

Brian's expecting a letter.
Fold the mailbox so that he's
ready to receive it!

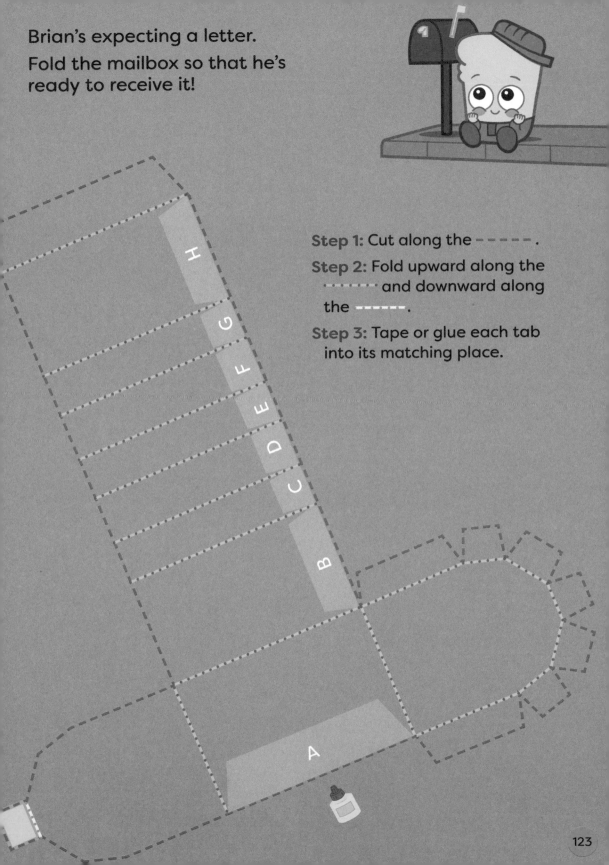

Step 1: Cut along the ‑ ‑ ‑ ‑ ‑ .

Step 2: Fold upward along the
· · · · · · · and downward along
the ‑ ‑ ‑ ‑ ‑ .

Step 3: Tape or glue each tab
into its matching place.

H
G
F
E
D
C
B
A

HEY, GROWN-UPS!

You can extend this activity by writing more letters together.
Keep the mailbox so that your child can write and receive mail!

WAY TO GO!
STICKER
124

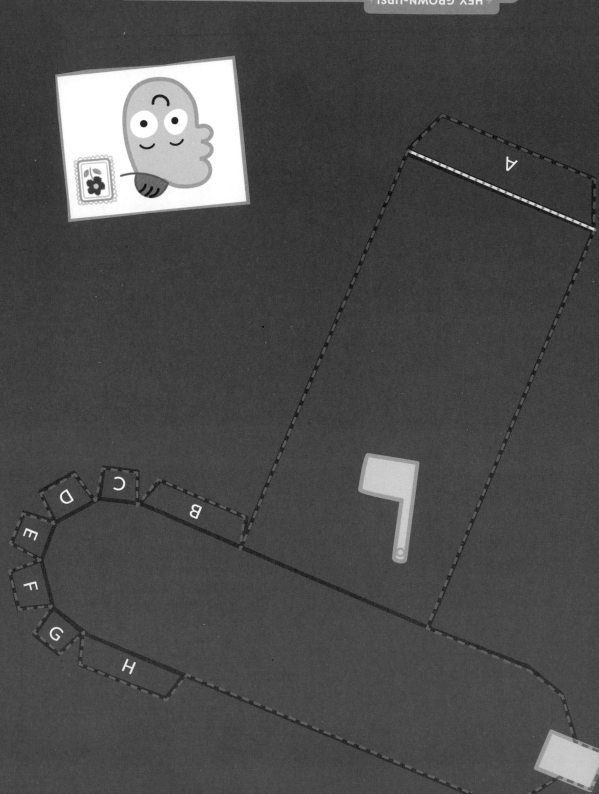

Let's **TINKER!**

Roll your paper. **Tear** it and **fold** it, too. **Bend** and **twist** pieces of paper. Do any of your actions leave marks? How does the paper change shape?

Scissors
(with an adult's help)

Construction paper

Glue or tape

Book

Let's **MAKE!**

A Mail Fort!

1. With the help of an adult, **cut** the construction paper into 2-inch-by-8-inch strips.

2. **Fold** each strip in half, and then again in half, giving you four equal sections.

3. **Fold** each strip into a triangle with an overlapping section.

4. **Glue** down or tape the overlapping section.

5. **Repeat** these steps to create the pieces for a wall!

★ HEY, GROWN-UPS! ★

This final project is just a bit more challenging than the others. Take it slowly and help your child with each step. This is a great opportunity for your child to practice focus and perseverance. And it's a perfect moment to praise them for their concentration and progress!

Let's **ENGINEER** a solution!

The MotMots are building a fort out of mail. They want to create a structure that will hold a book. **Think** of other shapes that they could use, like loops or cubes. See if you can make these shapes.

You're a TinkerActive CHAMPION!